Animal Builders

A Bee's Nest

Niles Worthington

Cavendish Square

New York

Published in 2017 by Cavendish Square Publishing, LLC
243 5th Avenue, Suite 136, New York, NY 10016

Library of Congress Cataloging-in-Publication Data

Names: Worthington, Niles.
Title: A bee's nest / Niles Worthington.
Description: New York : Cavendish Square, 2017. | Series: Animal builders | Includes index.
Identifiers: ISBN 9781502620828 (pbk.) | ISBN 9781502620842 (library bound) | ISBN 9781502620835 (6 pack) | ISBN 9781502620859 (ebook)
Subjects: LCSH: Bees--Juvenile literature. | Beehives--Juvenile literature. | Animals--Habitations--Juvenile literature.
Classification: LCC QL565.2 W67 2017 | DDC 595.79'9--dc23

Editorial Director: David McNamara
Editor: Fletcher Doyle
Copy Editor: Rebecca Rohan
Associate Art Director: Amy Greenan
Designer: Stephanie Flecha
Production Coordinator: Karol Szymczuk

Printed in the United States of America

Contents

Bees live in a **colony**.
A colony builds a nest.

Some build in the ground.
Some **bore** into wood.

7

Honeybees build in trees. Honeybees make **honeycombs**. They use wax.

9

Bees chew the wax.
This makes it soft.
They form wax **cells**.

The cells have six sides.
Honeycombs have
many cells.

Beekeepers put out boxes.
These are called **hives**.
Beekeepers take the honey.

15

Nests have one door. It is near the bottom. Bees guard the nest.

Honeybees stay inside in winter. They eat honey.

19

Bees may leave a colony.
They build a new nest.

21

New Words

bore (BOR) To make a hole in something.

colony (KAH-luh-nee) A group of bees living and working in the same place.

cells (SELZ) Sections of a honeycomb.

hive (HYVE) A place for bees to build a nest.

honeycomb (HUH-nee-kohm) A wax place where honey and young bees are kept.

22

Index

23

About the Author

Niles Worthington plays soccer and tennis and enjoys writing children's books. He works as a pharmacist and loves studying nature.

About BOOKWORMS

Bookworms help independent readers gain reading confidence through high-frequency words, simple sentences, and strong picture/text support. Each book explores a concept that helps children relate what they read to the world they live in.